John H. B. Latrobe

**A Lost Chapter in the History of the Steamboat**

John H. B. Latrobe

**A Lost Chapter in the History of the Steamboat**

ISBN/EAN: 9783337409647

Printed in Europe, USA, Canada, Australia, Japan

Cover: Foto ©Andreas Hilbeck / pixelio.de

More available books at **www.hansebooks.com**

**Fund-Publication, No. 5.**

# A LOST CHAPTER
### IN THE
# History of the Steamboat.

BY

J. H. B. LATROBE.

*Baltimore, March, 1871.*

PRINTED BY JOHN MURPHY,
PRINTER TO THE MARYLAND HISTORICAL SOCIETY,
BALTIMORE, MARCH, 1871.

# A LOST CHAPTER

IN THE

# HISTORY OF THE STEAMBOAT.

IN the spring of 1828, my law office was in the Athenæum building, so called, afterwards destroyed by fire. My business was scant, for I had but recently been admitted to the bar. I was ruminating, no doubt, upon my prospects, when the door was opened, and a handsome, elderly man, of distinguished presence, entered and asked me, in rich unctuous tones, and with a strong Irish accent, if my name was Latrobe, and if I recollected him. His face was familiar, and so was his voice; but I could not place him. Seeing that I hesitated, he said, "and it would be strange if you did, for you were but a bit of a child when you last saw me in your father's house. I am John Devereux Delacy," and he rolled out his sounding name as though he was proud of it. I recollected him then. Fourteen or fifteen years back it had been his fancy to pet me as a child. It was this that had impressed him on my memory. "Ah, you know me now," he said: "you remember when I used to be so much with Fulton and Roosevelt and Chancellor Livingston and Dr. Mitchell, at the Navy Yard house." This was the name given to my father's residence in Washington, not far from the Navy Yard. After recalling well remembered incidents and indulging in general remarks for a while, Mr. Delacy took a survey of my scantily furnished office, and said, "not overwhelmed with business, my young friend: so much the better for me: you will have the more time to attend to something I want you to undertake. If you succeed, it will be the making of both our fortunes. I want suit brought against every steamboat owner in the United States; and you must begin with old Billy McDonald, here in Baltimore. See this;" and, suiting the action to the word, my visitor drew from his breast pocket the original parchment letters patent, now before me, signed by James Madison, President, James Munroe, Secretary of State, and Richard Rush, Attorney General, granting to Nicholas J. Roosevelt the exclusive right to his 'new and useful improvement in propelling boats by steam.' Dated December 1st,

1814. The patent had still some months to run. The specification contained the following description of the improvement:

"In a boat or vessel of any form, but of sufficient capacity to contain the machinery, I place a steam engine of a power proportioned to the resistance to be overcome in propelling a boat or vessel a given distance in a given time. This steam engine is supplied by a boiler of the usual form, or made cylindric, one or more at pleasure, so as to be of sufficient capacity to feed the engine. I next place two wheels over the sides, on the axles of which I put fliers, dispense with them, or otherwise, contrive them at pleasure, either to regulate motion, or to give additional velocity; or, they may be connected with the valve shaft and steam engine by wheels, so as to give any number of revolutions that may be desired. The arms of the water wheels I would make of wood, to which I attach floats or paddles of cast iron or thick boiler plate sheet iron, though they may be made of wood. These floats I make move up and down on the arms by means of screws and holes, so as to make them deeper or shallower in the water, in taking a hold on the water, agreeably to the depth of the water the boat may draw, or the lading there may be on board, or agreeably to other circumstances. The supporters of the outer ends of the water wheel shaft to be made of iron with braces, though they may be made of wood, if required.

NICHOLAS J. ROOSEVELT.

Witnesses:

> JEREMIAH BALLARD,
> JOHN DEV'X DELACY."

Delacy watched me closely as I read the letters patent; and, I remember, placed his gloved finger on his own name at the bottom. I had not been carried away by his promise of a case. He was remarkably well preserved; but his habiliments approached what might have been called seediness; although his air and carriage would have borne up against even longer used apparel. It was easy to be seen that a contingent fee was all that could be expected: but the parchment, the accuracy of the description, its perfect correspondence with the steamboats in use, and its date, made the case look better than I had at first thought it would.

Taking the letters patent from me, Mr. Delacy placed in my hands a carefully prepared assignment from Roosevelt to William Griffith, an eminent lawyer of New Jersey, conveying them in trust for the benefit of Roosevelt, for one-third interest, of Delacy, for one-third, and of Griffith and Aaron Ogden, of a well known and distinguished family, for the remaining third. The assignment gave Griffith the power to sell rights and sue infringers; and excepted from its operation the Shrewsbury and Jersey Stage Company and Ogden, who were already licensees of Roosevelt, the latter running a boat between Elizabethtown and New York.

Nor was this all. Delacy, who evidently was pleased with the impression he saw he was making, next handed me an opinion on a case stated, given by Mr. Wirt, in 1826, of which the following is an extract:

## CASE.

In the year 1809, Robert Smith, Esquire, then being Secretary of State, an application was made to him by the late Robert Fulton, Esq., for a patent for the using of vertical wheels with steam engines or other power to propel boats through the water; but though he filed such his application, &c., he neither subscribed nor swore thereto in the manner prescribed, or required, by law; for the name, Robert Fulton, is in the handwriting of another man.

In 1814, (under view of the circumstances,) a patent was granted to Nicholas J. Roosevelt, for the using vertical wheels with steam engines, or other acting power, to propel boats, &c., through water, the patent or papers issued to Fulton being considered void, and but as so much blank paper.

Public notice was given of the patent having been granted to Roosevelt, and Fulton never urged his claim, but from that moment abandoned it; and Roosevelt's patent, though well and publicly known to exist, and to be in existence for twelve years, has been neither impeached nor impugned; neither does any other person lay claim to the invention of the application of vertical wheels.

It is asked, if, under the within stated circumstances, the patent to Roosevelt is not valid; and at this distance of time from being issued, is not now unimpeachable?

Other questions were asked in connection with the assignment. Mr. Wirt's answer to the above is alone important however at this time. It is as follows:

BALTIMORE, *July* 11*th*, 1826.

On the above statement I am of opinion, that the patent to Roosevelt is valid. It is still subject to impeachment, however, on the ground that he was not the first discoverer of the improvement which he has patented. The distance of time since the date of the patent is sufficient to bar a proceeding to set it aside by *scire facias* under the third section of the Act of 1793; but any defendant, against whom an action may be brought under the patent, may impeach it at any distance of time, under the sixth section of the Act of 1793.

Satisfied from this showing that Mr. Delacy's case was not a bad one, I agreed to undertake it, and wrote to Mr. Roosevelt, in the State of New York, upon the subject. He corroborated all that I had heard, sent me copies of important correspondence, and referred me to Richard S. Coxe, Esq., of Washington, who was the executor of Mr. Griffith, the assignee for the original papers. Mr. Griffith had then been for many years dead.

Among my clients, at this time, was the late Mr. John S. Stiles, who, hearing what had taken place with Delacy, agreed, in consideration of participating in my fee, to visit Washington, call on Mr. Coxe, obtain the Griffith papers, and afterward go to Clermont, the residence of the late Chancellor Livingston, who, I learned from Mr. Roosevelt, was connected with the investigation I was about to make.

On the return of Mr. Stiles to Baltimore, and after an examination of papers he had obtained, the case looked so strong, that I called on Mr. Wirt, reminded him of his opinion, shewed him my documents, and asked him if he would come into the case on a contingent fee. I called also on Mr. Taney. Both gentlemen thought the prospect of success was fair; and both agreed to participate in the trial, which was to take place in the Circuit Court of the United States, in Baltimore. It was thought best, on consultation, to begin the litigation by suing the company owning the steamboats running from Baltimore to Frenchtown, at the head of which was the late General William McDonald; and I addressed myself, at once, to as thorough a preparation as I was capable of making, prior to issuing a writ. Difficulties now presented themselves which I had not appreciated when Mr. Delacy called on me, or while gathering the documentary evidence. I am reminded of the first that occurred by Mr. Roosevelt's reply to my letter already mentioned. It was necessary that we should have a meeting; but to bring this about required an hundred dollars, which neither of us had to spare. Then, commissions were necessary to collect the testimony of parties at a distance. In a word, it was apparent that more means were needed than I, a young lawyer, just beginning the world, could command; and Mr. Stiles had spent all *he* could afford in his visits to Washington and Clermont. I was in trouble, too, about Delacy. He had procured, on credit, from Patterson, the then fashionable tailor in South street, a complete outfit; and not having the money to pay for it, Patterson, who was unwilling to wait until our success at law made my client's fortune, put him in jail, in spite of his sounding name and lofty bearing. I had to become security for him, and ultimately to pay the debt. By this time, I had found out that he had an aptitude for this sort of thing; and that it would be for my own advantage, and the credit of the great case, to get him out of town as soon as possible. Always buoyant in his feelings, gushing in his manner, and intending to be honest, he was one of those men who are always in trouble. As already intimated, therefore, I was not as hopeful at the end of some months as I had been; and, when Mr. Taney asked me, one day, how my preparation was getting on, I told him, candidly, all my troubles, present and prospective. His advice was kind and prompt. The case he still thought was a fair one, and if it went on he would go into it with earnest zeal: but, he advised me not to hamper myself in the commencement of my professional career. One thing was certain. I would have against me every steamboat owner in the United States. Now-a-days, combinations often carry on these great cases. It was not so then; and, after discussing the matter with Mr. Stiles, I tied up my papers, and abandoning the idea of suing General McDonald, placed them in the pigeon-hole, where, with a single exception, they have remained undisturbed for upwards of forty years, and now see the light, only that this

Lost Chapter may be written. The exception was this. In 1855 or 1856, I lent the package to Dr. Hamel, a Russian *savant*, who was about preparing a history of steam navigation, and who visited America to obtain information on this and other subjects. The papers remained in his hands for some months. They were returned when he was on the eve of departure for Europe. He has been dead for many years; and I am not aware that he made any use of what he got from me. It is probable, therefore, that what I am about to tell will be told for the first time, now. It seems proper that it should not be wholly lost, and hence I tell it.

To us, of to-day, it appears strange that the first suggestion of steam, as a motive power for the propulsion of vessels was not accompanied by a plan for using vertical wheels over the sides to which to apply it. And yet, this was very far from being the case. Fitch, in 1783, propelled a boat upon the Delaware by a steam mechanism that moved paddles, as an Indian works the paddle in a canoe. Rumsey had a vertical pump, operated by steam, in the middle of his boat, that drew in water at the stem and expelled it at the stern, through an horizontal trunk in the bottom. Dr. Franklin's plan was to make a current of steam propel the vessel as it issued from the stern. Then steam was applied to oars, and for a season a boat was rowed by steam between Philadelphia and Bordentown. Dr. Kensey built a steam engine that was to operate upon oars, paddles and flutter wheels. Fulton himself, as stated by his biographer, Colden, after subjecting Rumsey's mode to the test of calculation, "thought of paddles and duck's feet, abandoning which, he took up the idea of using endless chains with resisting boards upon them as propellers. His calculations," still using Colden's language, "giving him a favorable opinion of the mode; at least, he was persuaded it was greatly preferable to any other method that had been previously tried."

The above were notions, mere notions, all of them — all of them were utter failures; and the enumeration of them, now, excites our astonishment that any one of them should have been tried. Long before the day of Fulton, long before the earliest period to which Fulton, at any time, ever attempted to carry back the plan of steam navigation, it was, as I have shewn, entertained and practically experimented on, here in America, by Fitch, Rumsey, Kensey and others, all of whom failed to succeed. What made it a success at last? *The use of vertical wheels over the sides of the vessel.* Why had it not succeeded previously? *Because vertical wheels were not combined with steam power* in the production of the desired result—a successful steamboat, as now understood. The merit lies with him, therefore, who first suggested the combination that produced success,—describing it in such a practical shape that the task of invention was completed, leaving nothing to be done but the mechanical execution. Was this the merit of Robert Fulton? Unquestionably it was not; and the object of this writing is to demonstrate the fact.

I have before me the original "petition of Nicholas J. Roosevelt to the Honorable the Governor, the Councils and the Representatives, of the State of New Jersey, in Legislative assembly convened,"—dated January 13th, 1815, in which he "asserts (I quote his words) with the modest and manly firmness of honesty that he is the true and original inventor and discoverer of steamboats with vertical wheels now in use." And he prays from the Legislature, "as the constitutional guardians of the rights of their fellow-citizens and of the interests of the State," such privileges, as on examination and hearing he may be thought entitled to. At this time, there were vague notions of the powers of the States over their navigable waters, which the decision of the Supreme Court, in connection with the steamboat controversy, dissipated at a later day.

Belonging to an old New York family, whose worth had been illustrated then, as it has been since, by the honorable positions that its members have held in that great State, Mr. Roosevelt was a gentleman of character and education, of an active enterprising temper, and addicted all his life to matters connected with civil engineering and mechanics. Appreciated by all who knew him as a person of unblemished honor, his word was independent of his oath; but, attached to the petition just referred to is an affidavit, not without interest, of which the following is an extract:

"In or about the year 1781 or 1782, this deponent resided with a certain Joseph Oosterhaudt, about four miles above Esopus on the North, or Hudson river, in the State of New York. That he did at that time make very many actual experiments, as well upon mill machinery as upon the motion and buoyancy of bodies in and through water; and did then and there make, rig and put in operation, on a small brook near the house of the aforesaid Oosterhaudt, a small wooden boat or model of a boat with vertical wheels over the sides, each wheel having four arms or paddles, or floats, made of pieces of shingle attached to the periphery of the wheels whereby to take a purchase on the water; and that these wheels being acted upon by hickory and whalebone springs propelled the model of the boat through the water by the agency of a tight cord passed between the wheels and being re-acted on by the springs."

Soon after the evacuation of the city by the British, Mr. Roosevelt returned to New York; and following the bent of his inclinations, we find him, some years afterward, becoming interested in the Schuyler Copper mines in New Jersey, on the Passaic, then called Second river. Here he found some parts of an old atmospheric engine, which he used in completing a perfect machine of that description; and meeting with an engineer from the establishment of Bolton & Watt, whom he employed to make improvements, he built engines for various parties, and constructed for the water works in Philadelphia, the ponderous machines, which, for many years, supplied that city with water, by pumping from the Schuylkill into the distributing reservoir at Centre Square. During all this time, the subject of steam navigation seems never to have been lost sight of. He wanted to substitute for the hickory and whalebone of his Esopus experiment the mighty agent with whose multitudinous uses the world was then beginning to be familiar.

Among other persons who had heard of Mr. Roosevelt's views in this direction, was the late Robert R. Livingston, better known as Chancellor Livingston, who, on the 8th of December, 1797, wrote to him (I quote from the original letter now before me) as follows:

"Mr. Stevens mentioned to me your desire to apply the steam machine to a boat. Every attempt of this kind having failed, I have constructed a boat on perfectly new principles which, both in the model and on a large scale has exceeded my expectations. I was about writing to England for a steam machine, but hearing of your wish, I was willing to treat with you on terms which I believe you will find advantageous for the use of my invention."

The Chancellor was an inventor, but unlike most inventors was a man of large wealth; and the result of the correspondence, thus commenced, all of which is before me, was an agreement between the Chancellor, Roosevelt, and John Stevens of Hoboken, to build a boat on joint account, for which the engines were to be constructed at Second river by Roosevelt, while the propelling agency employed was to be on the plan of the Chancellor.

I have not been able to make out, from the very voluminous correspondence, the precise character of the Chancellor's contrivance; but I infer that it consisted of wheels with vertical axes, submerged at the stern, that forced a stream of water outward from between them, and so propelled the vessel. The inventor's own idea of it must have been vague in the first instance; for there is scarcely a letter to Roosevelt from the time the work was commenced, until it was abandoned, that does not suggest changes and alterations. Steam appears to have been applied to the machinery about the middle of the year 1798, unsuccessfully; and the Chancellor, charging the failure to want of power in the engine, proposes to throw the cost of it upon the builder. This is of course resisted. Further improvements in the propellers are made. The engine is then alleged to be *too* powerful: and so matters go on, until the 21st of October, 1798, when Roosevelt writes to the Chancellor, giving him an account of a trial trip, on which the speed attained was equivalent to about three miles in still water; though, with wind and tide, the Spanish Minister, who was on board and highly elated, estimated the actual speed at double that amount.

In the meanwhile however, on the 6th of September, 1798, Roosevelt wrote to the Chancellor an important letter in this connection, in which, after referring to a change in the plan, he says:

"I would recommend that we throw two wheels of wood over the sides, fastened to the axes of the flys (fly wheels) with eight arms or paddles; that part which enters the water of sheet iron to shift according to the power they require either deeper in the water, or otherwise, and that we navigate the vessel with these until we can procure an engine of the proper size, which, I think, ought not to be less than 24 inch cylinder."

No better description of a side wheel steamboat has ever been given than is contained in this letter of the 6th of September, 1798, the original draft of which, with all its interlineations, is now before me; *and this is the first practical suggestion of the combination which made steam navigation a commercial success*, that there is a record of in America; and this also, when, as late as 1802, four years later, Fulton, as we are informed by his biographer, had become assured, that endless chains and floats were alone to be relied on!

Receiving no reply to the suggestion, thus made, Roosevelt writes to the Chancellor on the 16th of September, 1798, saying: "I hope to hear your opinion of throwing wheels over the sides;" when the Chancellor answers: "I say nothing on the subject of wheels over the sides, as I am perfectly convinced from a variety of experiments of the superiority of those we have adopted."

Again, on the 21st October, in the letter giving an account of the trial trip with the Spanish Minister on board, Roosevelt says, "he would wish the Chancellor's wheels to be tried, contrasted with paddles on Mr. Stevens' plan, or with wheels over the sides, so as to ascertain the difference in the application of the power." To which the Chancellor answers on the 28th October, 1798, referring to the Stevens' paddles, "they are too inconvenient and liable to accidents to be used—AND, AS FOR VERTICAL WHEELS, THEY ARE OUT OF THE QUESTION!"

Roosevelt was at this time so strongly impressed with the plan that the Chancellor thus peremptorily put aside, that in a letter of the 21st to the same John Stevens already mentioned, who, as we have seen, was one of the partners in the adventure, he says, "I am firmly of opinion that a vessel may be propelled at the rate of *eight* miles an hour."

Not even the praise of the Spanish Minister seems to have been sufficient to vitalize the Chancellor's boat; and we are led to suppose that it was recognized by all as a failure; for Stevens, who seems to have had more influence than Roosevelt, persuaded the Chancellor to adapt the engine to his contrivance of a set of paddles in the stern, pushing the boat forward as they were made by a crank motion to rise and fall. A rough sketch of this contrivance in a letter from Stevens, dated July 15th, 1799, is before me. The experiment so racked the Chancellor's boat as to make it unfit for use altogether. We wonder now that such things could have been thought of even.

In Mr. Stevens' letter there is a passage that indicates the reliance that was placed on Roosevelt by this, the most practical of his associates, and shews him to have been the party on whose skill the others depended. He says:

"In the meantime, I would wish to determine on our plan for placing the paddles in the stern of the boat and provide immediately to put it in execution. You and Stoudinger (a young man brought up by Roosevelt, and who subsequently became Fulton's right hand man, and one of the first practical engineers in America,) and Smallman (another of Roosevelt's employees) must lay your heads together on this subject; and, as soon as you have fixed upon the plan you conceive will be most eligible, I wish you would take a ride down and communicate it to me; and, at the same time, I can give you the result of my cogitations."

The Stevens' paddles, until they shook the boat to pieces, were far more successful than any one of the Chancellor's inventions; and I remember, distinctly, seeing a boat propelled by paddles in the harbor of New York, as I crossed the Hudson on my way to West Point, in the fall of the year 1818. The paddles I refer to, however, were on the sides, and not at the stern, and were literally paddles, being square floats attached to upright shafts, which a crank motion caused to rise and fall.

It is not difficult to understand why the Chancellor told Roosevelt that his vertical wheels were not to be thought of, and why Stevens, confessedly a man of ability and mechanical ingenuity, preferred his own suggestion. They doubtless believed that the percussion of the floats of the vertical wheel as they strike and then enter the water, and before they exert their greatest power; which is when they are at right angles with the surface, was objectionable and would be fatal to their usefulness. They feared also, most probably, the further loss of power consequent upon the lifting of the water as the floats emerged from it; and, wedded to their own schemes, they refused to subject the matter to the test of experiment. The paddles of Stevens, and the floats on the endless chains, to which Fulton gave the preference, entered the water perpendicularly, or nearly so, and were free from what was regarded, it is to be supposed, as the objection to Roosevelt's vertical wheels over the sides. That both Stevens and Fulton were wrong, and that Roosevelt was right, time has conclusively established.

Unwilling to abandon the idea of steam navigation, even after so complete a failure, the Chancellor devised still another plan, which was executed under Roosevelt's direction at the works on the Passaic, of the details of which I have no account. In this Roosevelt had no interest. It proved a failure. From all that I can gather, from the documents in my possession, the efforts here described were made in 1798, 1799 and 1800, almost uninterruptedly, and were controlled by the Chancellor, who was, evidently, the moneyed man of the concern, and whose dictum, as we have said, was regarded as conclusive by his associates. So promising did the matter seem after Roosevelt had commenced the engine for the boat, that, in March, 1798, the Legislature of New York, granted the Chancellor, "the exclusive right of navigating all boats that might be propelled by steam on all the waters within the territory, or jurisdiction, of the State for the term of twenty years, provided he should, within a twelvemonth, build such a boat, the mean of whose progress should not be less than four miles an hour." The month of March, 1799, elapsed, however, without the condition of the grant having been complied with. At a later date, a similar grant was made to Livingston and Fulton.

In the latter part of the year 1800, Mr. Jefferson appointed the Chancellor minister to France, where he remained until 1804, having in the meanwhile negotiated the treaty which ceded Louisiana to the United States, and where he made the acquaintance of Robert Fulton. In 1804, the Chancellor made the tour of Europe, and returned the following year to the United States.

In Colden's Life of Fulton, there is an account, in the Chancellor's own words, of the commencement of his acquaintance with Fulton. I quote: "Robert R. Livingston, Esquire, when minister in France, met with Mr. Fulton, and they formed that friendship and connection with each other to which a similarity of pursuits generally gives birth. He communicated to Mr. Fulton the importance of steamboats to their own country; informed him of what had been attempted in America, and of his resolution to resume the pursuit on his return, and advised him to turn his attention to the subject."

We have already seen that Mr. Fulton's plan, after making calculations as to the efficiency of paddles and ducks' feet, was to use endless chains with resisting boards upon them as propellors. With these he made a course of experiments on a little rivulet that runs through the village of Plombiéres, in France, in 1802; and "addressed several letters to Mr Livingston and Mr. Barlow, giving them a minute account of his experiments and assurances of the certainty of success which they afforded him."

That the Chancellor had informed Fulton of what had been attempted in America, is admitted by Colden; and this, too, prior doubtless, to the experiments at Plombéires. That Roosevelt's pertinacity in regard to wheels over the sides was communicated with other information is not to be doubted; that the Chancellor should have told him, as he told Roosevelt, in the letter of October 28th, 1798, "that they were not to be thought of," it is most reasonable to suppose; and that Fulton agreed with the Chancellor is proved by the "assurance of certain success" which he entertained, of endless chains and floats, or resisting boards.

Between the spring of 1802 and the fall of that year, Mr. Fulton changed his mind; for he and Livingston were building a boat, propelled by Roosevelt's vertical wheels, in January, 1803. The Chancellor, by this time, had become convinced that vertical wheels were things "to be thought of." That it was Roosevelt's plan that was adopted after all their own plans had failed—the plan derived, with the details of its execution, from Roosevelt himself,—does not seem to admit of any reasonable doubt.

Biography is too often eulogy. The name of Fulton is irrevocably, and justly, the representative name in connection with steam navigation throughout all lands. For a while, and in the memory of the writer, the name of Livingston was connected with it in men's mouths. But Livingston's connection with the subject is fast being forgotten. Fulton's never will be forgotten, not because he was the inventor of the steamboat however, not because he first suggested the combination that made success certain; but because, in his hands, it became a commercial success. He was the first who demonstrated its practical utility, when, in 1807, he made the first voyage in the Clermont from New York to Albany and back. Still he was indebted to others, in the first instance, for the elements of his success.

I have said that biography is too often eulogy. The biographer becomes jealous of the reputation of his hero. Colden was not exempt from the weakness common to his class; and instead of giving to Roosevelt the credit of having first put the idea of vertical wheels over the sides into a practical shape, by his detailed description of their mechanism, he says that the want of success of a French inventor, who had horizontal screws on either side of a boat, "it is probable," induced Mr. Fulton again to resort to the wheels, which, in the original paper that he communicated to Lord Stanhope, in 1793, he proposed to use as propellors. Even had this been so, without any question having arisen as to the facts, Roosevelt's model of a boat at Esopus, with its hickory and whalebone springs, would have been ten years ahead of the Frenchman.

But there are some matters connected with the letter to Lord Stanhope, which are not without interest in this connection.

We have seen that Roosevelt, in January, 1815, applied to the Legislature of New Jersey, for protection as an inventor of the vertical wheels over the sides, for which he had obtained letters patent from the United States in the preceding month of December, 1814, being the original document shewn to me by Delacy. Somewhere about this time, Mr. Fulton appeared as a witness before the Legislature in connection with this same subject of steam navigation; and Colden's life contains a letter from Mr. Emmet, the celebrated lawyer, in which he states, that, in order to shew Mr. Fulton's prior claim to invention, in the application of "water wheels to steamboats," he examined him to prove a copy of the letter in question. Nothing was said, it would seem, of its being a copy, when this was first presented: but Governor Ogden noticed that the letter was written on *American paper;* and, subsequently, Mr. Fulton explained that the first copy having been considerably worn out and obscured, he had copied it over again and attached it to the old drawings. This was made the subject of uncomfortable criticism by the opposite counsel; and Mr. Emmet, in his letter, expresses great indignation at what he states was a malicious attempt to injure the honor of the dead, and regrets that he omitted to notice, in his reply, the insinuations which Mr., afterwards Judge, Hopkinson permitted himself to make. The occurrence was unquestionably an unfortunate one, whatever the real facts may have been; and respect for the memory of Mr. Fulton leads me to hope that Mr. Emmet was correct in his version of the transaction. His letter, however, is important in another aspect: it shews that the merit of the invention, at the time, was considered to be the application of vertical wheels over the sides, and that this was claimed for Fulton on the strength of the letter to Lord Stanhope and the accompanying drawings of 1793, notwithstanding the endless chains and floats already referred to as illustrating the convictions of 1793.

I have never seen the drawings or read the letter of Mr. Fulton; but it is difficult for me to believe that he had invented in 1793, what was unquestionably the solution of the difficulty, and yet, in 1802, have dwelt in his letters to Livingston and Barlow upon his assurances of the certainty of success with endless chains and resisting boards. It is with no want of charity, that it is suggested, that Mr. Colden, in writing a biography, overlooked the possibility of its logic being criticized when compared with its facts.

There is some light, however, to be obtained from Lord Stanhope's reply to Mr. Fulton's letter. It is as follows:

"HOLDSWORTHY DEVON, *October 7th*, 1793.

"SIR: I have received yours of the 30th September, in which you *propose to communicate to me the principles of an invention which you say you have discovered respecting the moving of ships by the means of steam. It is a subject on which I have made important discoveries*. I shall be glad to receive the communication which *you intend*, as I have made the principles of mechanics my particular study, &c." (There are no words italicised in the original. L.)

Certainly, it is only necessary to read this letter to be satisfied, that the one to which it is a reply, and it is not suggested that Mr. Fulton ever wrote another, could not have described the combination which made the steamboat the thing that it now is: or that it could have been accompanied by drawings shewing the plan finally adopted,—the Roosevelt plan, going back as far as 1782, and described in practical detail in the letter of 21st October, 1798.

It is true that Mr. Fulton obtained letters patent of the United States for his steamboat in 1809— in reference to which Mr. Colden says, as though to corroborate Fulton's claim as inventor,

"They (the Chancellor and Mr. Fulton) entered into a contract, by which it was, among other things, agreed that a patent should be taken out in the United States in Mr. Fulton's name, which Mr. Livingston well knew could not be done without Mr. Fulton *taking an oath that the improvement was solely his.*"

And a patent was in fact taken out, in those days when patents were had for the asking, and when none of that examination, which now protects the public, was required by law.

We have already seen, in the case stated for Mr. Wirt's opinion, the allegation that Fulton neither subscribed nor swore to the specification; and that the name Robert Fulton was in the handwriting of another man. Unless this had been the fact, it would hardly have been alleged in a paper, prepared for the opinion of eminent counsel. But I have before me an original letter dated Trenton, January, 1815, addressed to Mr. Roosevelt by Delacy, in which the latter gives an account of the proceedings before the Legislature, and in which is this sentence:

"Fulton has the effrontery to avow his having got Fletcher to sign his name and makes light of it, as if he was entitled to violate the laws, as well as private rights, at pleasure."

It is true, this is the letter of a partizan in a struggle before the Legislature. Still, the matter of fact would not be misstated in a private correspondence, where there was no conceivable motive to mislead.

The committee of the Legislature finally reported, and very wisely, that it was inexpedient to make any special provision in connection with the matter in controversy before that body.

It was in March, 1815, on the heel of the Legislative proceedings, that the deed of trust to Mr. William Griffith was made, and the fact of his accepting the trust, and that Aaron Ogden of New Jersey, was a party to the transaction, shews that the cause of Roosevelt as the inventor of vertical wheels over the sides under the patent of 1814, was deemed good as against the patent granted to Fulton four or five years previously. Had the letter to Lord Stanhope or the reply thereto, been regarded by the outside world, or by those interested in the subject, as sufficient to establish Fulton's prior right to the invention of vertical wheels over the sides of steamboats, counsel of the standing of Mr. Griffith would not have become mixed up in the business, licenses to use Roosevelt's patent would not have been granted, nor would I have made the acquaintance of John Devereux Delacy; for Roosevelt's pretensions would have been nipped in the bud.

My tale is nearly ended. The object has been to shew that the merit of the practical suggestion of the employment of vertical wheels over the sides of steamboats was due to one who has been lost sight of in this connection, and wholly ignored in the biography of Fulton, who availing himself of the suggestion of another, in all its details, made it a great commercial success, and in so doing built upon it a lasting fame. That the papers I have referred to, now collated for the first time, shew this to be the fact, I think there can be no question.

It may be interesting to state something in regard to the subsequent career of Roosevelt. He was once asked why, with the secret of success in his possession, he allowed it to slumber. Why did not *he* anticipate the Clermont in the first five years of the present century. I give the answer in his own words from a manuscript before me.

"*First*: At the time Chancellor Livingston's horizontal wheel experiment failed, I was under a contract with the corporation for supplying the city of Philadelphia with water, by means of two steam engines; and, besides, I was under a contract with the United States to erect rolling works and supply government with copper, rolled and drawn, for six 74 gun ships, that were then to be built. The engines for the supplying of Philadelphia with water I completed, though with heavy loss. The rolling works I also brought into operation upon a very extensive scale, and a considerable quantity of copper was delivered. But the encouragement from government by which I had been led into this heavy expense was cut off by a change of men in the administration. The 74s were laid aside, and no appropriations were made, and embarrassment to me was the natural consequence."

This embarrassment, in the then condition of the law, was imprisonment for debts contracted in getting ready to fulfil his contract. In truth, he was a broken man. In the meanwhile, on the return of Livingston and Fulton to America, the workmen that Roosevelt had brought from Germany and made what they were, entered into Fulton's service, and to their skill was he indebted for the mechanical success of his earlier boats. In 1807, Roosevelt was introduced to him; and in a letter from the Chancellor, now before me, references to old times are pleasantly made; and, a year or two afterwards, we find Roosevelt associated with Fulton in the introduction of steamboats on the Western waters. Here, he built the New Orleans, the pioneer boat that descended the river in 1811—the year of the comet and the earthquake. The voyage of the New Orleans is, in itself, a romance; but time does not permit it to be told at present.* With all his merit, Fulton was not an easy man to get along with; and Roosevelt had his faults of temper too, no doubt; and after the successful voyage of the New Orleans, the two men parted, and Roosevelt disappeared from public life, and was lost in the quiet of the domestic circle of a numerous and happy family. He died at a very advanced age, not many years ago, forgotten by the world as he was forgotten by the biographer of Fulton. He appears again before me, as I write, as I remember to have seen him in my childhood, and in after years—a finished gentleman, energetic and sanguine, warm and generous in his temper, a devoted husband and father, and now made the hero of a lost chapter in the history of the steamboat.

*Somewhere about the year 1842, the writer of the foregoing address was narrating the substance of it at the White Sulphur Springs of Virginia. Among his hearers was Mr. Samuel Davis, of Philadelphia, but formerly of Natchez, Mississippi, who supplemented the story with the following anecdote. He was standing on the wharf at Natchez, one of a crowd, watching the approach of the New Orleans on her first voyage. There was a rise in the river at the time; and when the steamboat rounded to, to head up stream, she was some short distance below the landing,—and, for a while, the current was more than she could overcome. At Mr. Davis' side, was an old negro servant, who watched the struggle with much excitement, slapping his thighs and gesticulating in a most outlandish way. When at last, after a more rapid revolution of the wheels started the boat ahead, the negro threw up his hat, exclaiming, " By golly. Sa, old Massesseppa got her massa; hooraw." Mr. Davis sent a quantity of his cotton by the boat to New Orleans, against the advice of all his friends. He was the first person who ventured a bale on such a risk!

# APPENDIX.

### N. J. ROOSEVELT TO R. R. LIVINGSTON.

PROPOSES VERTICAL WHEELS WITH THE SIZE OF CYLINDER AND PRESSES FOR MONEY ARRANGMENTS.

SECOND RIVER, *Sept. 6th*, 1798.

DR SIR,

I have your two letters of the 31st and 1st inst. before me. Since writing you the 27th, I made an experiment in order to ascertain as nearly as I could the power of the engine, and put on your wheels. This was done by laying the vessel on shore stern foremost so as to leave the wheels entirely out of the water. The Engine was then put to work at the rate of from 40 to 45 strokes and wheels turned from 160 to 180 revolutions per minute. When the water first entered them it was thrown out with great violence; but before it got any considerable depth in them the motion of the engine was impeded and in a short time entirely stopped. By this experiment I was fully convinced that the wheels would require a power far greater than this engine possesses and that any attempts to proceed with the power we have and the present wheels would be fruitless. I was also farther convinced (by getting men whose strength was ascertained to turn the wheels by hand before the operation of the engine) tho' she has her full power and indeed considerably more than as first mentioned, I expected we would have. Now, Sir, to proceed with the experiment you recommended of closing the openings with doors will be doing nothing more than what we have already done by the last trial. I WOULD THEREFORE RECOMMEND THAT WE THROW TWO WHEELS OF WOOD OVER THE SIDES FASTENED TO THE AXES OF THE FLYS WITH 8 ARMS OR PADDLES, THAT PART WHICH ENTERS THE WATER OF SHEET IRON TO SHIFT ACCORDING TO THE POWER THEY REQUIRE EITHER DEEPER IN THE WATER OR OTHERWISE AND THAT WE NAVIGATE THE VESSEL WITH THOSE UNTIL WE CAN PROCURE AN ENGINE OF PROPER SIZE WHICH I THINK OUGHT NOT TO BE LESS THAN 24 INCHES CYLINDER. The Barometer to ascertain the exact power of the engine has not as you observe been left to depend entirely on Mr. Van Ness, although I looked upon him as your Representative according to the tenor of your own letter; but Mr. Mark and Mr. Speyer have both been on the search for one and have not yet succeeded. The copper pipe for it is made and we will I believe be obliged to wait for the glass until we can get it from the glass house above Albany. I have requested Mr. Speyer, who has gone up to the Oneida country, to call on Mr. Dezang for that purpose. If you know of any to be had in New York please to inform me and I will immediately get it.

As to your charge of my want of candor and my possessing too much distrust, those Sir are charges which have never before been laid to me and which I feel perfectly free from and I will recommend to the Chancellor to meet me in future upon equally candid and fair ground. I can assure him he shall never have reason to complain of me on that score again.* We have as you observe put our hands to the oars and ought not to look back until we reach port. This I am for, Sir, with all my heart, and firmly believe that with this determination we have nothing to fear, as I think, *with the wheels I have recommended*, that the State patent may be secured. We will then have time to prepare for your wheels, and if they should not have the effect you promise us, we can then adopt such other plans as we may together think best. No bad consequences need be apprehended from what I communicated out of your letter to Smallman and Stoudinger as they are as anxious for the success of the business and your good opinion as I am. As to altering any of the wheels in the way you propose I cannot approve, as the alteration will be attended with considerable expense, and as I believe any alteration we can make with our present small Engine will be inadequate to driving the wheels to any advantage. In this the Chancellor will agree with me when he considers that when the Engine making 30 strokes per minute the horizontal wheels make 120 revolutions by which $\frac{3}{4}$ is taken from the power to afford this.

I sincerely hope that Mrs. Livingston may soon recover from her accident so that you may not be detained long from thoroughly investigating everything appertaining to our present concern.

I am, dear Sir, &c., &c.      N. J. ROOSEVELT.

N. B. I have not, upon overlooking what I have above written, been so particular in my objections to your proposed alterations as may be agree-

---

*The reference here is to a letter of the Chancellor (numbered 25 in the collection I have,) in which, being then in a dissatisfied and complaining mood, he says: "I again repeat, Sir, that I trust in a few days to hear that experiments have been made and to be minutely acquainted with the result, that I may take my measures accordingly. In doing of which should wish to receive your advice. From a frank and candid communication much more advantage will result to all parties than from reserve, silence and distrust.      I am, dear Sir, your most obt. hum. serv't,

See letter of Aug. 31, 1798.      R. R. LIVINGSTON.

able and will ask for a little of your patience. See how the alteration of the wheels on the connecting rod by being smaller will operate. They will most certainly shorten the stroke of the engine. This therefore cannot take place unless we alter the wheels round which they move accordingly, which may be done. At the same time in doing it we shall be obliged to lengthen the spindle of the horizontal wheels and disturb the wooden work the whole of which will be attended with considerable expense and require a second alteration when we come to operate with power equal to what those wheels will require, and indeed, why should we go to any expense in alterations which can do us no service; as I clearly saw from actual experiment that about 1400 pounds will be necessary to be applied directly to the wheels independent of friction, which is equal to an engine of 24 inches Cylinder. An Engine of this size I find has 5424 pounds power independent of the friction of the machine and I think power enough for the air pumps (perhaps something more.) This I cannot however ascertain until I get a barometer and try our present engine, which I believe perfect. I was about trying the power by weights but found difficulties which I have not yet been able to get over, as her power is equal both ways, and to bring the weight only to the connecting rod would tear everything to pieces.

Yours, &c.     N. J. ROOSEVELT.

A plan of my substitute which may not be quite correct, as I do not understand anything of drawing.     N. J. R.*

---

## N. J. ROOSEVELT TO R. R. LIVINGSTON.

Second River, Sept. 10th, 1798.

Dear Sir,

I acknowledge receipt of yours of the 3d Inst. By this time you have doubtless recd. mine of the 6th Inst. which gave you all the information on the subject of the boat I was then capable of doing; since which I have thought of trying another experiment upon *the present plan* and concluded to morrow to set about it. It will take us three days with two hands which will cost very trifling and enable us to calculate with more certainty what power will be required *for your wheels.* The plan is this. Sun and planet wheels we will take off and form a double crank with the coupling links, which at one end will be fastened to the shaft of the fly wheels by taking out the brasses and drilling holes for pins to enter. This change will give us only half the motion of your wheels we first contemplated and

---

* The plan here referred to is not among the papers. L.

consequently double the power we now have. I will try this in the same way we did the last time by leaving the vessel's stern on shore, and in the meanwhile *I hope to hear your opinion of throwing wheels over the sides. I will also be glad* to know if it is more agreeable to you to give a note for the balance of your proportion of the expense attending this business or whether you will make me a remittance in cash. Could I at present raise money through the house of J. Mark for all the ends I have in this quarter I would not solicit more money until you come down. This however it is not for them to do. I hope the Chancellor will consider my situation in the midst of many workmen as an apology and pardon me for my impatience.

         Yours, &c.    N. J. ROOSEVELT.
R. R. Livingston.

## R. R. LIVINGSTON TO N. J. ROOSEVELT.

ACKNOWLEDGES WHEELS OVER THE SIDES TO HAVE BEEN PROPOSED BY ROOSEVELT AND REJECTS THEM.

             CLERMONT, 18*th Sept.*, 1798.
DEAR SIR,

Mr. Mouchette is just returned. I sincerely congratulate you upon the success of the engine of which he gives the most favourable report & fully justifies yr. confidence in your engines. I am sufficiently sanguine to hope that all difficulties are now vanished. Knowing our power nothing remains but adapt the vessel to it. In attempting this hitherto we have deceived ourselves by wandering into the field of conjecture rather than adhering to plain calculations & we shall still do so if we expect that the present engine will turn the wheels we now have 80 times in a minute, as will appear from this calculation. Our wells contain exactly 60 cubic feet of water. The whole of this is set in motion at every revolution of the wheels with a rapidity equal to the main motion of the arms, that is if the wheels make 80 revolutions in a minute at the rate of 8 miles an hour. Now as the boat will not remove more than 20 feet of water if she goes 8 miles an hour, if it was possible to move the wheels as they are now constructed 80 rounds in a minute we should throw away one half of our power, for the boat could not move faster than the water in the wheels & the power would be uselessly expended in throwing out water unnecessarily.

But it will be found on experiment that however perfect our engine is, it cannot turn the present wheels 80 times in a minute. The wheels then must necessarily be altered or the motion rendered still slower. To make the motion slower is to diminish our chance of moving the boat fast because she will at no rate move faster than the water in the wheels though she may be made to move as fast as I have found on actual experiment. The wheels then must be altered, not by making the arms shorter for this would diminish their motion, besides that it would require an alteration in the boat—but by diminishing their depth. They are now if I recollect 18 Inches deep, let them be reduced to nine Inches.

Let the motion of the wheels by no means exceed 80 nor be lower than 70 turns in a minute and I will answer for the success of the experiment, & upon the whole it will turn out a fortunate discovery since we shall find that our wells need not be above half the size we have made them & of course much room and much weight of water be saved in future. That we have erred hitherto should not discourage us. It is the fate of all new undertakings and it is happy when the error can be so easily discovered & detected. Another circumstance of considerable moment must be attended to. If the diminution of the motion is brought about by changing the sun and planet wheels, one half the motion of the flys will be lost & they rendered almost useless from this circumstance. If they are made heavier they will overload the boat.

I would propose as the best mode of altering the motion of the wheels to alter the cog wheels & to leave the sun and planet wheels as they were—this will give the proper motion to the fly & diminish the friction. Let the cog wheels be made smaller and have no more cogs than the trunnel rounds, or only so many more as will serve to give the motion we require. Nor will this alteration be attended with more trouble than the one at first proposed; but even if it is, it is so essential to give the flys a rapid motion that we must, now we have gone so far, submit to this trouble and expense to have this experiment properly made. *I say nothing on the subject of* WHEELS OVER THE SIDES *as I am perfectly convinced from a variety of experiments of the superiority of those we have adopted.* I expect to be down the last of this month when I shall see you & make such money arrangements as we may find necessary.

In the meantime I hope to hear how you go on. I flatter myself no delay will be incurred which can possibly be avoided, every moment being precious. Mr. Mark will I hope forward this to you the moment it arrives, so that the necessary alterations may be made before you proceed far on any difficult plan.

I am very much hurt that you should construe any part of my former letters into a reflection on your candour. I am sure that nothing of this kind was ever intended & I flatter myself that if you attend a little more to the expressions (tho: I cannot now recollect them) that they will not bear this harsh construction.*

I am dear Sir, with esteem, your most ob: hum: servt:

ROB. R. LIVINGSTON.

## N. J. ROOSEVELT TO R. R. LIVINGSTON.

### Experiment made & Opinion of the Spanish Minister—Again Coaxes to have Vertical Wheels tried.

SECOND RIVER, *Oct. 21st*, 1798.

DEAR SIR,

I dropped you a line in haste on Friday last, since which I received your favour of the 10th: the person to whom you gave it in charge did not put it in the post office until yesterday. Your instructions therefore came too late for the rims, as they had by your former request been left off and no bad consequence has resulted. I have not yet seen Mr. Stevens, but have been expecting him every day, as he requested me by letter to inform him what time we would be ready, which I did. Had I received your letter sooner I would also have sent to see if Mr. Mouchet was still at N. Ark & requested him to come up.

There was no occasion to try the wheels from 5 Inches upwards, as I found the Engine overloaded at 5. I think at present the most advisable mode of proceeding for us will be to change the wheels on shaft and spindle so as to give the Engine her full speed with 50 revolutions of the lower wheels, and if she will carry more, then increase the width of the paddles. I have ordered a pattern made for two wheels accordingly and will cast them the first casting we make after it is finished. Please to write me if you agree in this respect. The Spanish Minister was on board the day we made the last experiment and was perfectly well pleased with the operation of the Engine and will give us an order for one of 36 Inches. This will cost him upwards of 13,000 Dolls: Our small one is not equal to the purposes for which he wants his. During our sail he, at the time the tide and wind favoured us, supposed we went at the rate of 6 miles an hour; but I think the delight he felt expressed at the novelty of the Voyage was the cause of his mistake. My report to you was three miles, still water, which I have reason to believe was accurate. I have at present a better opinion of your plan than ever, and could wish them to be contrasted with paddles upon

---

*The Chancellor had evidently forgotten the concluding paragraph of his letter of August 31, 1798.

Mr. Stevens' plan, OR WHEELS OVER THE SIDES, so as fairly to ascertain the difference of the application of the power. We have by the last experiment a striking proof in favor of your plan which is demonstrated by the diminution in width and slow motion of the wheels. At our last experiment the effect was certainly greater than we could have promised ourselves.

I hope to hear from you soon, and in the meanwhile will do what strikes me as reasonable upon our present plan so that no time is lost.

Mrs. Mark requests me to thank you for your polite invitation of visiting Mrs. Livingston, but does not think it will be in her power this fall, as Mr. Mark is at present too much occupied with business to leave home.

Yours respectfully,      N. J. ROOSEVELT.

This letter is complim'y to Livingston—about his plan of wheel—but still Roosevelt mentions that it would be prudent to try in contrast *Stevens' paddles*—(& his *own* plan) wheels *over the sides*. (Note by Judge Griffith.)

---

## R. R. LIVINGSTON TO N. J. ROOSEVELT.

### LIV'N ACKNOWLEDGES THE BOAT TO ANSWER & REFUSES TO USE VERTICAL WHEELS.

CLERMONT, 28 *Octr.*, 1798.

DEAR SIR,

After sending mine of yesterday I received your favor of the 21st, in which you enter more particularly into the experiments you have made, but not so fully as I would wish, as you will find by the queries I have troubled you with. If you are right as to the motion through the water, the Spanish Minister could not err much in his calculation, for it appears to me that the tide in your river is not short of 2 miles & I have found in my models that the velocity of the boat with the tide is greater in proportion than the mere difference between that and still water.

This is one of the experiments I wished you to ascertain accurately by running one hour with the tide & determining the distance and running back the same distance against the tide. Be it as it will, we now know what we can do with a sufficient power, and tho' *paddles should even do more they are too inconvenient and too liable to accidents to be used*—AS FOR VERTICAL WHEELS THEY ARE OUT OF THE QUESTION.

What I principally write now for is to ask you whether it would not be better instantly to fit the boat for passengers by putting a deck over so much as you make cabbin of. This should be the whole, only leaving room for wood near the engine. This deck should be of inch pine boards

& rounded so as to carry off the water and made as tight as possible. It should be raised about ten Inches so as to admit of glasses that shove past each other all round The inside only wants to be papered with any cheap common paper and to have two rows of benches the one behind the other. The rear bench so low as to admit the knees under the front one. A narrow table of one board should run through the middle. The back cabbin should be fitted for the ship's company and have windows and shutters in case of bad weather. Some arrangement should also be made for boiling in pot and kettle. All this should be going on while you are fitting the machinery. It will I believe be best to get two or three quick hands from New York to do it as your shipwright is both slow and extravagant. We have yet one month to use and a pretty important one, because the roads will soon be bad, and tho' we should only go 3 miles an hour we shall still be able to pick up something besides our expenses and acquire some experience of what further is necessary. I have provided a Captain at £5 a month who understands the river. You say you have a steward and fire engine hand. Tho' I think Smallman should make the first voyage.

     I am, Dr. Sir,     R. R. LIVINGSTON.
Mr. N. J. Roosevelt.

The headings of the foregoing letters are copied from their respective indorsations which would seem to have been made by different hands and as though in the preparation of a case. L.

---

### PATENT TO MR. ROOSEVELT.

### THE UNITED STATES OF AMERICA,

*To all to whom these LETTERS PATENT shall come:*

WHEREAS, NICHOLAS J. ROOSEVELT, a Citizen of the United States, hath alleged that he has invented a new and useful improvement

### IN PROPELLING BOATS &c. BY STEAM,

which improvement he states has not been known or used before his application; hath made oath that he does verily believe that he is the true inventor or discoverer of the said improvement; hath paid into the Treasury of the United States the sum of thirty dollars, delivered a receipt for the same, and presented a petition to the Secretary of State, signifying a desire of obtaining an exclusive property in the said improvement, and praying that a patent may be granted for that purpose: THESE ARE THEREFORE to grant, according to law, to the said NICHOLAS J. ROOSEVELT, his heirs, administrators, or assigns, for the term of fourteen years, from the first day of December, one thousand eight hundred and fourteen, the full and exclusive right and liberty of making, constructing, using and vending to others to be used, the said improvement; a description whereof is given in the words of the said Nicholas J. Roosevelt himself, in the schedule hereto annexed, and is made a part of these presents.

IN TESTIMONY WHEREOF, I have caused these Letters to be made Patent, and the Seal of the United States to be hereunto affixed.

[SEAL]

GIVEN under my hand, at the City of Washington, this first day of December in the year of our Lord one thousand eight hundred and fourteen and of the independence of the United States of America, the thirty-ninth.

JAMES MADISON.

*By the President.*

JAS. MONROE, *Secretary of State.*

CITY OF WASHINGTON, *to wit:*

I DO HEREBY CERTIFY, That the foregoing Letters Patent were delivered to me on the first day of December in the year of our Lord, one thousand eight hundred and fourteen to be examined; that I have examined the same, and find them conformable to law; and I do hereby return the same to the SECRETARY OF STATE within fifteen days from the date aforesaid, to wit; on this first day of December in the year aforesaid.

RICHARD RUSH,
*Attorney General of the United States.*

TO ALL TO WHOM THESE PRESENTS SHALL COME:

*Nicholas J. Roosevelt, of the State of New Jersey, Esqr. sends greeting:*

BE IT KNOWN, That I, the said Nicholas J. Roosevelt have discovered, invented and constructed a new & useful mode & improvement in the propelling of boats or vessels through water by the force & agency of fire & steam, the construction of which discovery, invention & improvement is specified as follows, as the mode to which I have given a preference reserving to myself the right of varying and changing the proportions and combinations of the several parts of the said discovery and invention as experience may suggest or as I shall think advisable or expedient, to wit.

A true copy from the Specification filed in the Patent Office.

GEO. LYON, *Clk.*

PATENT OFFICE, *3d December,* 1814.

*THE SCHEDULE referred to in these Letters patent and making part of the same containing a description in the words of the said Nicholas J. Rooscrelt himself of his improvement in propelling Boats, &c. by steam.*

In a boat or vessel of any form, but of sufficient capacity to contain the machinery required, I place a Steam Engine of a power proportioned to the restance to be overcome, in propelling a boat or vessel a given distance in a given time, this steam Engine is supplied by a boiler of the usual form or made Cylindric one or more at pleasure so as to be of sufficient capacity to feed the Engine. I next place two wheels over the sides, on the axis of which I put flyes, dispence with them or otherwise combine them at pleasure, either to regulate motion or give additional velocity, or they may be connected with the water shaft and steam Engine, by wheels so as to give any number of revolutions that may be desired. The arms of the water wheels I would make of wood, to which I attach floats or paddles of cast Iron, or of Boiler plate thick sheet Iron, though they may be made of wood. These floats I make move up and down on the arms, by means of screws and holes, so as to make them enter deeper or shallower in the water, in taking a purchase or hold on the water agreeably to the depth of water the boat may draw, and the lading there may be on board, or agreeably to other circumstances. The supporters of the outer ends of the water wheels shaft to be made of Iron with braces, though if required they may be made of wood.

Ns. J. ROOSEVELT.

Witnesses: Jere'h Ballard,
John Dev'x DeLacy.

---

Of the foregoing correspondence, but a small portion relates to the question of wheels over the sides. It is inserted at length however,—going, as it does, to shew the warm interest, and the active measures that were on foot at the close of the eighteenth century to develope one of the mighty agencies of the nineteenth. The crudeness of many of the suggestions and the literary carelessness of the correspondence on both sides, is indicative of a very different condition of things from that which exists at present. L

www.ingramcontent.com/pod-product-compliance
Lightning Source LLC
Chambersburg PA
CBHW030710110426
42739CB00031B/1539